United States Electric Lighting Company

The Maxim Electric Light and Power Co.

Philadelphia

United States Electric Lighting Company

The Maxim Electric Light and Power Co.
Philadelphia

ISBN/EAN: 9783337270483

Printed in Europe, USA, Canada, Australia, Japan

Cover: Foto ©Andreas Hilbeck / pixelio.de

More available books at **www.hansebooks.com**

THE MAXIM

ELECTRIC LIGHT AND POWER CO.

PHILADELPHIA.

— ✣ —

OFFICERS:

President:

WM. G. WARDEN.

Vice-President:

WM. L. ELKINS.

Secretary and Treasurer:

F. M. NICHOLS.

General Manager:

L. P. THOMPSON.

Directors:

WM. G. WARDEN,	HENRY L. DAVIS,	H. C. FRANCIS,
WM. L. ELKINS,	M. MALONEY,	P. A. B. WIDENER.
	G. L. McKELWAY,	

Executive Committee:

P. A. B. WIDENER,	H. C. FRANCIS,	G. L. McKELWAY.

— ✣ —

GENERAL OFFICE:

617 & 619 ARCH STREET,

PHILADELPHIA.

The Maxim Electric Light & Power Co. holds exclusive licenses for the State of Pennsylvania under all patents owned by the United States Electric Lighting Co., and for this territory has the exclusive right to furnish the apparatus described in the following illustrated catalogue.

For price lists, estimates, and full information in regard to apparatus, apply at the General Office of the Company, 617 & 619 Arch Street, Philadelphia.

Oct. 16, 1882.

THE UNITED STATES ELECTRIC LIGHTING COMPANY.

— ✦ —

GEORGE W. HEBARD, President.

MARCELLUS HARTLEY, 〉
ANSON PHELPS STOKES, 〉 Vice-Presidents.
CHARLES R. FLINT, 〉
LEONARD E. CURTIS, Secretary.
LOUIS FITZGERALD, Treasurer.

Trustees :

GEORGE W. HEBARD.	
MARCELLUS HARTLEY	of Hartley & Graham.
ANSON PHELPS STOKES	of Phelps, Stokes & Co.
CHARLES R. FLINT	of W. R. Grace & Co.
LOUIS FITZGERALD	Prest. Mercantile Trust Co.
HENRY B. HYDE	Prest. Equitable Life Assurance Society.
ROBERT B. MINTURN	of Grinnell, Minturn & Co.
D. B. HATCH	of Hatch & Foote.
D. C. WILCOX	Prest. Meriden Brittannia Co.
THOMAS H. HUBBARD	of Butler, Stillman & Hubbard.
LEONARD E. CURTIS	

— ✦ —

ILLUSTRATED CATALOGUE, 1882.

— ✦ —

Business Office :

EQUITABLE BUILDING, No. 120 Broadway, New-York.

Factory : Newark, N. J.

INTRODUCTORY.

THE United States Electric Lighting Company was organized in 1878, and was among the first in this country to undertake the development and introduction of the Electric Light for purposes of practical illumination. The Weston Electric Light Company, which is now owned by this company and under the same management, was organized a year earlier, and several of the inventors and electricians who are now employed by the United States Company, and whose inventions and patents have become its property, had done a large amount of valuable preliminary work long before the organization of either company.

Within the past few years lighting by electricity has grown from a doubtful experiment into an established system of illumination, in large and rapidly increasing practical use; and in the work by which this result has been accomplished this company has taken an active part. Having abundant capital, it has been able to employ inventors and electricians of the highest ability, to furnish them with extraordinary facilities for experimental work and investigation, to secure the control of important inventions made by other inventors, and to provide extensive manufacturing facilities for constructing its apparatus in the most perfect and economical manner.

Mr. WESTON, Mr. MAXIM, and Professor FARMER are the principal electricians of the company, and the apparatus which it manufactures has, for the most part, been invented by them. Other inventors and electricians, of well-recognized ability, have also been employed, and valuable outstanding patents have been purchased from time to time.

The ablest counsel and experts in the country have been employed by the Company to take charge of all patent matters relating to its business, and great pains have been taken, not only to thoroughly protect by patents the work of its own inventors, but to carefully avoid infringement of the rights of others.

The company now owns or controls more than a hundred and fifty patents, and is constantly adding to this number as its inventors make further improvements. These relate chiefly to the electric light, electro-plating, and electrical transmission of power, and cover the most important contributions made to the progress of these applications of electricity during the past twenty years.

As is well known, there are two principal systems of lighting by electricity — the voltaic arc system and the incandescent system. While other companies have given their exclusive attention to one or the other of these two systems, this company has undertaken the development of both, believing that the greatest advantages would be secured by working the two together. The arc light is especially adapted for lighting large spaces where a great amount of light is required, but is not suitable for general interior illumination. The incandescent light is especially adapted for interior lighting, as it admits of more convenient division and distribution; but it is greatly inferior to the arc light in economy for lighting large spaces. In many cases the best results can be obtained only by a combination of the two systems.

The Weston arc system and the incandescent system, comprising the Maxim incandescent lamp and the Weston machine, which have been adopted by the company, have long since passed the experimental stage, and are in extensive practical use both in this country and abroad. They have received the highest commendations, both from eminent scientific men and from practical users, and the large and rapidly increasing demand for apparatus for lighting by these systems is the most satisfactory evidence of the estimation in which they are held by the public.

It has been the policy of the company to spare no trouble or expense in securing the best forms of dynamo-machines, electric lamps, and other apparatus, and in perfecting them in all their details. Very important improvements have recently been made, by which greater simplicity of construction, and higher efficiency and reliability in operation have been secured. As such apparatus has to be used, for the most part, by persons having little or no practical knowledge of electricity, it has been the aim of the company to make its apparatus strong and simple in construction, and self-regulating, as far as possible, in operation, so that it can be operated without difficulty by any person with the most ordinary knowledge of mechanics. In this respect, as well as in efficiency, economy, and reliability in operation, and in the color and steadiness of the light produced, these systems of lighting are confidently believed to be far superior to any other now before the public.

In addition to its principal business of manufacturing electric lighting apparatus, the company does a very large business in electro-depositing apparatus. This branch of the business was established by the Weston Company, and has been very successful. The Weston electro-depositing machine has gone more largely into use than any other in the market, and has in all cases given the most satisfactory results.

Electric motors and various forms of special apparatus, and instruments for use with large currents, are also manufactured by the company.

Since its acquisition of the Weston factory at Newark, N. J., the company has concentrated its manufacturing business there. The capacity of this factory has been more than quadrupled during the past year, and it has been fitted up in the most thorough manner with the best modern tools and machinery. It is one of the largest

Factory of the United States Electric Lighting Co., Newark, N. J.

and best appointed factories in the country devoted to electrical work. A large force of skilled workmen is employed, many of whom have been with the company for a long time, and have been thoroughly trained in the manufacture of its apparatus. Only the best materials are used, and great precautions are taken to insure the most accurate mechanical and electrical work.

Various subsidiary or local companies have been organized in different parts of the country, under licenses from this company, and all are in successful operation. Among these are the New England Weston Electric Light Company, of Boston, Mass.; The Rhode Island Electric Light Company, of Providence, R. I.; The Connecticut Electric Light Company, of New Haven, Conn.; The United States Illuminating Company, of New-York City; The Newark Electric Light and Power Company, of Newark, N. J.; The Maxim Electric Light and Power Company, of Philadelphia; The Rochester Electric Light Company, of Rochester, N. Y.; The United States Electric Illuminating Company, of Charleston, S. C.; The Citizens' Electric Light Company, of Toledo, O.; The Cincinnati Electric Light Company; The Swift Electric Light Company, of East Saginaw, Mich.; The St. Paul Electric Light and Power Company, of St. Paul, Minn.; The Racine Electric Light and Power Company, of Racine, Wis., and many others.

These companies are using and introducing the apparatus manufactured by the parent company, and many of them are doing a large business in furnishing lights on rental from central stations.

ADVANTAGES OF THE ARC SYSTEM.

THE superiority of the Arc light over all other systems of illumination for use in places where a large amount of light is required, has been thoroughly demonstrated by experience, and is now generally well recognized.

First. It is the *cheapest* artificial light known. This has been shown both by scientific tests and by the experience of practical users given in the testimonials which we publish farther on.

Second. It is the *safest* light known, being wholly free from all danger of explosion, leakage, use of matches, etc., incident to gas, oil, and other systems of lighting. The underwriters throughout the country have made a careful examination of the subject, and have in all cases concluded that lighting by this system is free from danger, when the apparatus is properly constructed and erected. The New York Board of Fire Underwriters has adopted regulations for the erection of plants, with which we carefully comply.

Third. It is a *pure white light,* in character closely resembling sunlight. All colors appear precisely the same by this light as by daylight. This is a point of great importance where artificial light is used in factories, stores, dye-houses, and other places in which it is desirable to distinguish colors.

Fourth. It is an *agreeable* and *wholesome* light. A single gas-burner consumes as much oxygen as is required by five or six persons for respiration, and the noxious gases and great amount of heat evolved by oil and gas lights are disagreeable and deleterious to health. The electric light does not depend on combustion for its illuminating effects, and, accordingly, does not vitiate the air, and the amount of heat produced is extremely small. The light produced by the Weston arc system is *remarkably steady,* free from flickering, and is soft and agreeable to the eye.

Fifth. The *immense quantity* of light which can readily be produced by the arc system renders it possible to obtain a *perfect general illumination* of a workshop, store, or other large space which is not economically attainable by any other system of lighting. This is of great importance in manufacturing establishments where night work is necessary, as the work can be carried on with almost as much facility by the electric light as by daylight.

The arc system is especially adapted for lighting streets, public squares, parks, docks, and other out-of-door places, and for lighting large interior spaces, such as factories, mills, foundries, mines, warehouses, stores, public halls, railway stations, hotel offices, tunnels, and the like. Although it is not suitable for general interior illumination where only a comparatively small amount of light is required, the arc light is, within its proper field, far superior to all its competitors. With improvements in apparatus the field of the arc light is constantly expanding. The steady and reliable Weston arc lights are now in common use both in this country and abroad, in places where the flickering and uncertain arc lights of two or three years ago would not be tolerated, and are giving the most satisfactory results.

THE WESTON ARC SYSTEM.

THE Weston Arc System differs from other arc systems now in use, not only in the construction of the apparatus, but in the character of the current used and in the quality of the light produced. The lamps are adjusted to work with a shorter arc or separation between the carbon points, and the machines are constructed to generate a continuous current of lower electro-motive force and greater quantity than in other systems. This not only obviates the danger of accident to persons using the apparatus, but renders the light produced of *better quality* and of *greater quantity* for a given expenditure of power. While numerous fatal accidents have occurred from the use of machines producing an intermittent or pulsating current of very high electro-motive force, *no person has ever been in any way injured by the current from a Weston Machine.* This remarkable immunity from accident is not by any means fortuitous, but is due to the construction of the apparatus and the character of the current used in the Weston system. The electro-motive force of the current, even with a very large number of lights in circuit, is too low to permit it to injuriously affect any person accidentally coming into contact with the conductors, and the current is continuous and entirely free from the pulsations to which the disastrous effects of the current upon the person injured have been largely due in such accidents as have occurred with other systems. With our larger machines we have adopted additional precautions, in thoroughly insulating all parts which have to be handled, and we believe that the entire safety of the Weston system will commend itself as by no means an unimportant advantage.

The flickering due to slight impurities in the carbons, which is so noticeable in long arc systems, is almost entirely obviated by using a short arc, and the color and quality of the light are greatly improved. The light is free from the excess of blue and violet rays so noticeable in most other systems, and which are so disagreeable and trying to the eyes, and the light is much more diffusive.

The extreme delicacy of the feeding mechanism in the lamps, and the purity and uniformity of the Weston carbons, render the light remarkably steady, and the extraordinary efficiency of the machine secures the highest degree of economy.

In addition to the machine and the lamps, the Weston arc system comprises various auxiliary or supplementary devices, such as regulators, indicators, cut-off boxes, switches, and fixtures, which add greatly to its convenience and reliability.

THE WESTON DYNAMO-ELECTRIC MACHINE.

THE mechanical and electrical details of the Weston dynamo-electric machine have been very carefully studied, and we believe it is unrivalled in *efficiency, simplicity of construction, strength, durability, the ease with which it can be repaired in case of accidents, and excellence of workmanship and materials.* We invite a critical examination and comparison of this machine with any other, by skilled mechanics, or other persons conversant with the requirements of the art. It is beyond doubt the most symmetrical, substantial, and efficient machine in the market.

The general construction of this machine is shown by the cut on the opposite page. The field magnets are placed in a horizontal position on each side of the armature, and their cores, pole-pieces and yoke-plates form a rectangle of cast-iron which serves as the frame of the machine. The yoke-plates at each end are carried down so as to form feet, which support the machine, and the supports for the armature bearings are cast in one piece with the frame.

The armature is cylindrical in form, and its iron core is built up of a series of iron disks placed side by side, but separated slightly from each other. This construction is shown in the cuts on page 10, in which also a single disk is shown.

In this way the armature core is split up into a large number of separate sections insulated from each other by air spaces at every point (except very near the center).

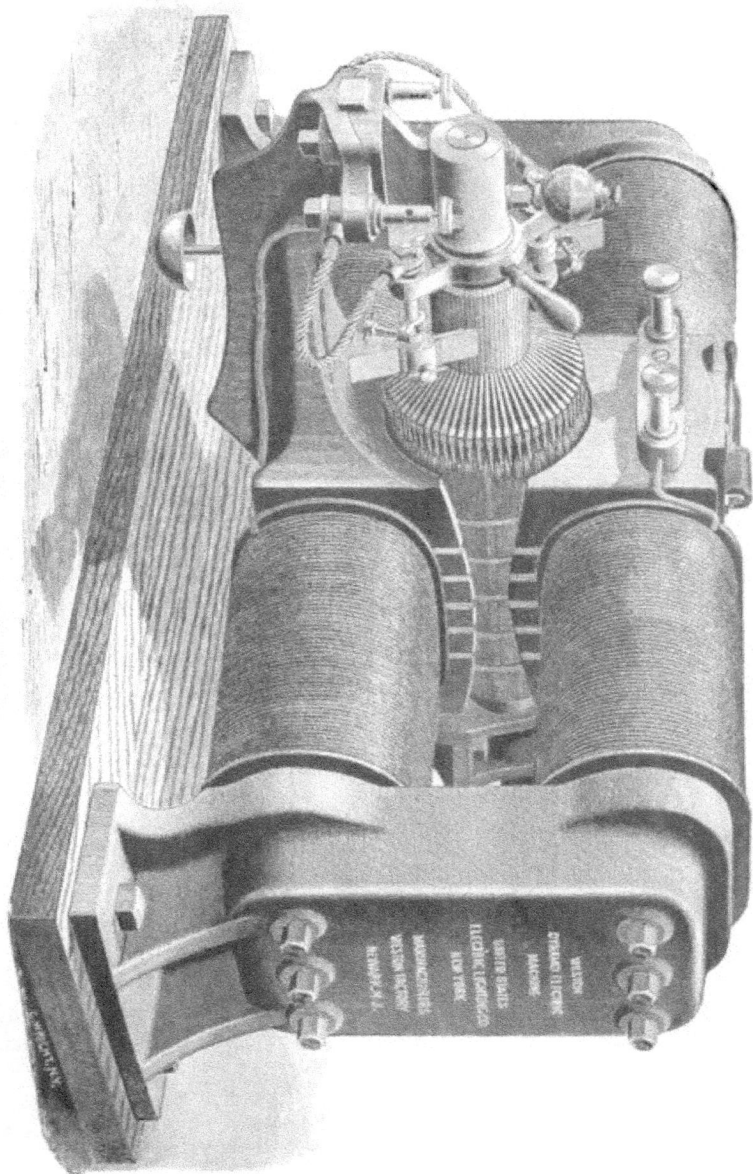

The Weston Dynamo-Electric Machine.

By this peculiar construction of the armature, induced currents in the core are almost entirely prevented, and the loss of energy and consequent injurious heating of the core, so common in other dynamo-electric machines, is entirely avoided.

In order to still further increase the efficiency of the machine, the armature is constructed to operate as a fan or blower to produce a rapid circulation of air from the center to the periphery, through the sectional core, thus cooling the conductors on the armature, and keeping their resistance much lower than would be the case if this method of construction were not used. The coils are wound lengthwise of the armature, and connected to the commutator at the end. The complete armature is shown in the cut below. By the peculiar winding of the coils on the armature, and

Armature Core and Single Disc.

Armature Complete.

their connection with the commutator, the highest possible efficiency is secured, and the coils are so perfectly balanced electrically that the spark on the commutator is hardly appreciable.

Owing to the rigidity of the bearings and general excellence of design and workmanship, the armature can be revolved between the poles with an extremely slight clearance—a condition very favorable to high efficiency.

The coils exciting the field magnets, instead of being placed in the main circuit in the usual way, are placed in a branch or derived circuit of high resistance, and only a very small fraction of the entire current passes through them. Great advantages are secured by this arrangement of the field coils. Less current energy is expended in sustaining the field, the current is more steady, and the machine more uniform in its operation; it is impossible to injure the armature by short circuiting the main circuit, and a perfect and extremely economical system of regulation can readily be applied.

The regulator is shown in the cut on this page. It consists of a rheostat or adjustable resistance placed in the field circuit. This is inclosed in a box, and is operated by a handle outside, as shown in the cut. It may be placed in any convenient position, either near the machine or at a considerable distance away. By simply turning the handle of the regulator, the machine may be adjusted to run any number of lights from one up to the full number it is capable of running.

All other methods of regulation which have been applied to machines for running arc lights have proved so objectionable in practice that they have been but little used. They have so disturbed the electrical balance of the machine as to produce a very injurious spark on the commutator with less than the full complement of lights in circuit, and the consumption of power has not been reduced at all in proportion to the number of lights cut out. With this method of regulation, however, the operation of the machine is as perfect with one light in circuit as with the full number, and the consumption of power is at all times very nearly proportional to the number of lights in use. A device for accomplishing the same result automatically is now in the works.

Regulator.

The efficiency of this machine is extremely high. Recent tests have shown that over NINETY PER CENT. of the power applied at the driving-pulley is available as useful current in the working or lamp circuit. No other machine in the market approaches this degree of efficiency.

We make machines of this type of various sizes, for running from one to thirty arc lamps in the same circuit. Machines of larger sizes are in course of construction, and will soon be ready.

Attached to all our derived circuit machines is a device for preventing shocks and sparks while establishing or breaking connection between the machine and the field conductors. This device consists of a coil of high resistance in the field circuit, in combination with a switch, which, when closed, cuts out the resistance coil. On opening the switch when the machine is in operation, the current is reduced to such an extent that the line connection may be broken without the least danger to the machine or to the person operating it.

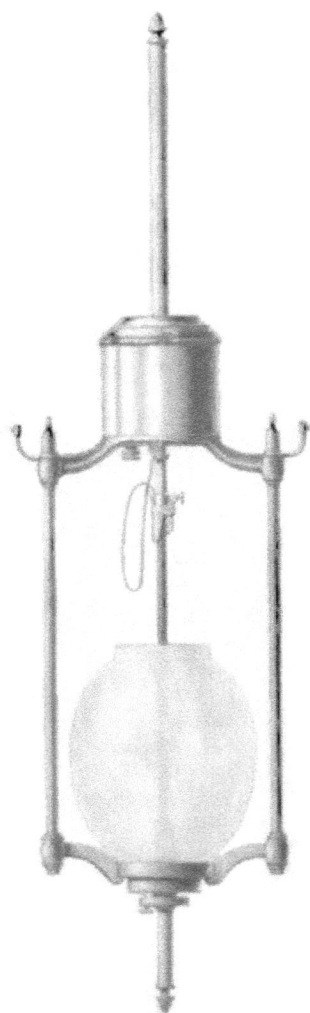

Plain Open-frame Arc Lamp.

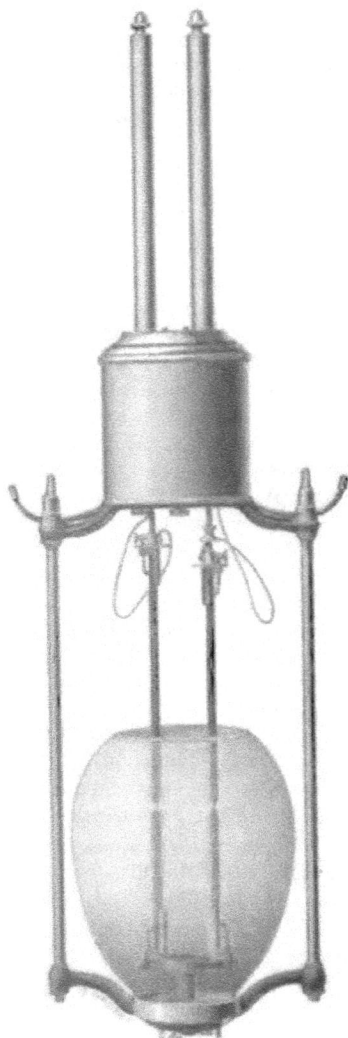

Duplex Arc Lamp.

ARC LAMPS.

WE furnish arc lamps of various forms for use with these machines. Some of these are shown in the cuts on this and the following page. In all these the lower carbon is fixed, and the upper carbon only is fed downward. The feeding mechanism is located in a casing above the arc, and works on substantially the same principle in all.

The lamp shown at the left, on page 12, is a plain, open-frame Weston lamp.   At the
right is shown a duplex lamp.   In this there are two sets of carbons so arranged that,
when the first set is consumed, the second
set is automatically brought into operation,

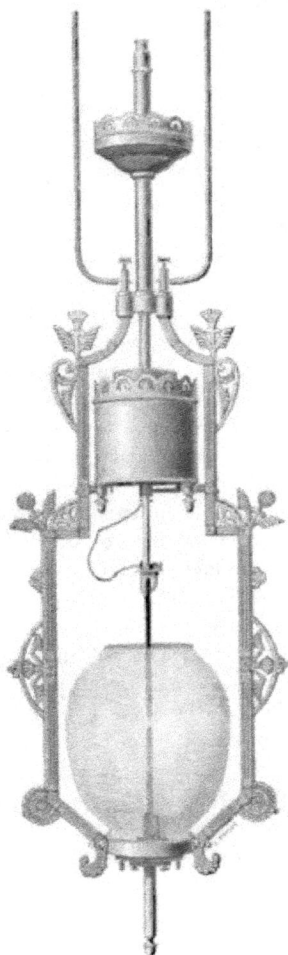

Ornamental Arc Lamp.

Inclosed-frame Arc Lamp.

and the feeding mechanism is at the same time transferred to them.   Lamps of this
type burn from sixteen to eighteen hours without renewal of the carbons.   In all
these lamps the frame is made of brass and iron, and all the electrical connections are

placed inside of the frame and thoroughly insulated from it. On page 13, at the left, is shown an ornamental lamp for use in stores, hotels, offices, and like places. On the same page at the right is shown an inclosed-frame lamp especially adapted for out-of-door use. The globe is suspended from the casing containing the feeding mechanism by means of a tubular support which incloses the upper carbon and the electrical connections. By this construction all the working parts of the lamp are entirely inclosed and thoroughly protected from the weather, the arc also is completely inclosed, and more perfect insulation is secured, both of the electrical connections and of the carbons themselves, than is attainable by any other construction. The same style of frame may be used for duplex lamps.

These lamps are especially designed for series lamps, as the feeding mechanism of each lamp is entirely independent, in its operation, of that of other lamps in the same circuit. They work equally well, however, as single lamps.

For use with reflectors in steamboat and head-light projectors and the like, we make a focusing lamp shown in the cut on this page. In this lamp both carbons are movable, and their relative rates of movement are so adjusted that the arc is maintained at a fixed point.

The feeding mechanism of the Weston lamp is *simple* in construction, and extremely *sensitive* and *certain* in operation. It maintains the proper adjustment of the carbon points with almost mathematical precision, and responds immediately to the slightest fluctuations in the strength of the current.

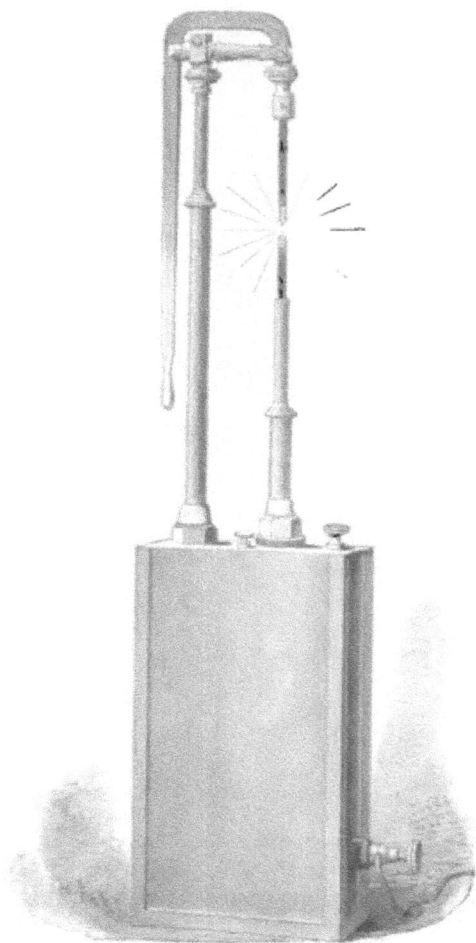

Focusing Lamp.

AUTOMATIC CUT-OUT.

WHEN lamps are run in series, two different forms of automatic cut-out are used with each lamp for shunting the lamp out of circuit, in case the feeding mechanism should for any reason fail to act. One of these consists of an electro-magnet placed in the circuit of each lamp, and so arranged as to close a shunt about the lamp whenever the circuit through it is for any reason interrupted, thus preventing the extinguishing of the other lamps in the series. The other form of automatic cut-out (shown in the cut on this page) is especially designed to prevent any injurious elongation of the arc through failure of the feeding mechanism to work properly. It consists of a spring switch normally held open by a small plug, made of an alloy which fuses at a very low temperature. This plug is placed near the upper carbon, but at a sufficient distance above the arc to prevent its melting when the arc is of normal length. If, however, the feeding mechanism fails to act, the arc becomes elongated as the carbons burn away, and the great increase of heat melts the fusible plug, allowing the switch to close and cut the lamp out of circuit. The cut-out may be again adjusted by opening the switch and inserting another fusible plug. A top view of the fusible plug, and the jaws holding it, is given in the lower part of the cut, at the right. This device has been found far more effective and reliable in operation than any other form of cut-out now in use, but, owing to the simplicity and certainty of action of the Weston feeding mechanism, it is rarely brought into action in practice.

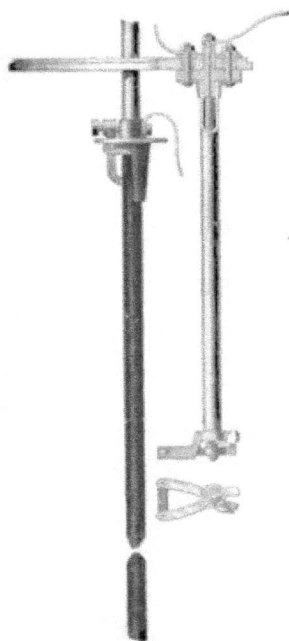

Fusible Plug Cut-out.

Time-meter.

TIME-METER.

THE cut at the right on this page shows a time-meter, especially designed for use where lamps are run from central stations. It can be applied to any arc lamp, and indicates the time during which the lamp has been in operation. This is very convenient where lights are rented by the hour.

INDICATOR.

THE indicator shown in the cut on this page is especially designed for use in central stations, or other places where lights are run at a considerable distance from the machine. It is included in the same circuit with the lamps, and, when the normal current is flowing, the needle of the indicator stands at zero; but should the current from any cause be increased or diminished, the needle of the indicator shows the direction of the variation, and rings an alarm-bell to attract the notice of the attendant.

Indicator.

CUT-OFF BOX.

THE cut-off box shown in the cuts below is also designed for use in lighting from central stations or in other places where the lamps are not located in the same building with the machine. It is placed in the circuit at the point where the line wires enter the building, and, by simply pressing a key shown in the centre of the cut, the lamps in the building are cut off the circuit, which, however, is still maintained intact through the other lamps. By pressing another key shown in the lower right-hand corner, the lamps are again placed in circuit. An indicator in the center of the box shows whether the circuit in the building is on or off.

Cut-off Box (open).

Cut-off Box (closed).

CARBONS.

THE steadiness and purity of color of the arc light are affected greatly by the *quality of the carbons used.* We have paid much attention to the manufacture of carbons, and have recently obtained improved machinery and introduced important improvements in the processes of manufacture, by which we are enabled to furnish users of our apparatus with carbons superior in purity, density, and uniformity of structure, to any others in the market.

PROJECTORS FOR STEAM-BOATS AND STEAM-SHIPS.

THE cuts below show projectors for use on steam-boats and steam-ships. The Ocean Projector consists of a parabolic reflector mounted upon trunnions and a swivel in such a manner that it can be readily turned in any direction, either horizontally or vertically. It is fitted with a powerful focusing lamp, and projects a very intense beam of light for a long distance. This has been in use for a long

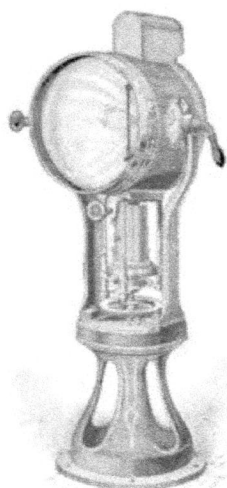

Ocean Projector.

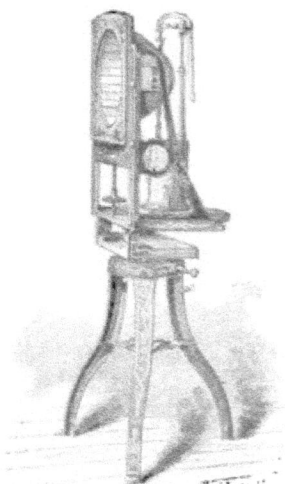

River Projector.

time on ocean steam-ships, and has been found to be of great service in navigation. The lamp can be readily removed from the frame for use on the vessel or about the dock, in loading or unloading. The River Projector, as shown by the cut, is of a somewhat simpler and cheaper form.

THE INCANDESCENT LIGHT.

IN the character and quality of the light produced the incandescent system is the most perfect means of artificial illumination yet devised. In this system the light is produced by the incandescence of a slender carbon conductor inclosed in a vacuum in a small glass globe, and is absolutely steady and uniform. The incandes-

2

cent light has all the advantages of the arc light in safety and convenience, and is superior in steadiness and color, and more soft and agreeable to the eye. This system is especially adapted for interior illumination where comparatively small lights are required, as it admits of indefinite division and distribution of the current. Although it has not the capacity of the arc system for producing large lights, and is greatly inferior to it in economy, the incandescent light has already demonstrated its ability to compete successfully with gas and other systems of lighting, in many places, and is destined in the near future to supplant gas for purposes of general interior illumination.

OUR INCANDESCENT SYSTEM.

IN this system the *Weston Dynamo-Electric Machine* and the *Maxim incandescent lamp* are used. The Weston machine for incandescent lighting is in its general construction similar to that already described for arc lighting, but the winding of the armature and field magnets is somewhat modified for producing the different quality of current required. One very novel and important feature of this machine is its *capacity for self-regulation*. As the number of lights in circuit varies, it is necessary to vary the quantity of the current generated in order to prevent accidents to the lamps, and to keep them at a uniform brilliancy. This has been accomplished in other systems by manual adjustment of the machine from time to time by an attendant. This is obviously objectionable, as it involves the presence of an attendant at the machine, and accidents may occur, and in fact do occur in practice, from lack of attention. Mr. Maxim has devised an ingenious regulator for accomplishing this result automatically, which has attracted much attention and works well in practice. Mr. Weston, however, has been able, by a peculiar construction of the machine itself, to make it *entirely self-regulating* without the use of any special mechanism. This operates with such quickness and precision, that, with one hundred lights, for example, in circuit, ninety-nine may be instantly turned out without affecting the brilliancy of the remaining light, and without any change in the adjustment of the machine. *This is the only machine ever produced which accomplishes this most desirable result.* In cases where it is desirable to vary the illuminating power of the lamps, a regulator similar to that used with the arc machines is supplied. This, however, is not used where the lights are always run at the same candle-power. The efficiency of this machine is even higher than that of the arc machine of the same type, and it is in all respects far *superior to any other machine in the market.*

The Maxim incandescent lamp, which is shown full size in the cut on the next page, consists of an M-shaped carbon conductor, inclosed in a vacuum by a glass globe about two and one-half inches in diameter. The carbon is made by a peculiar process devised by Mr. Maxim, which gives it very great durability, strength, and

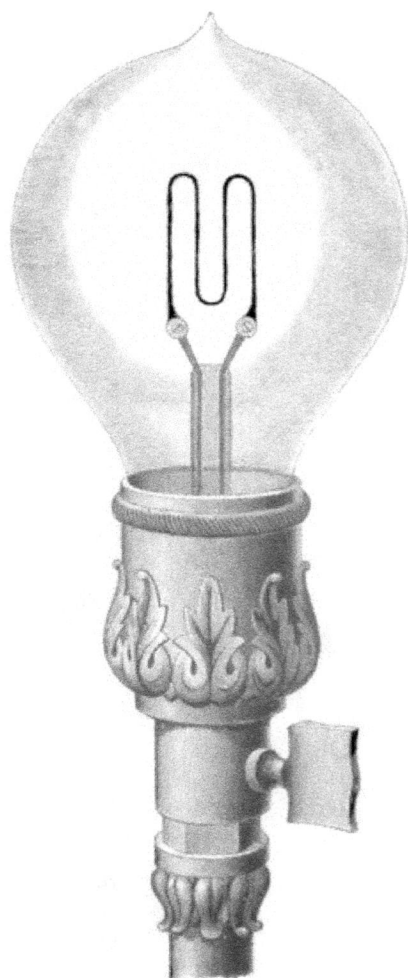

The Maxim Incandescent Lamp.

capacity for withstanding the disintegrating **effect of** powerful currents.   One of the Maxim lamps, constructed to **give** a light of twenty-five candles, was run for a short time at the Paris Exposition at an illuminating power of eleven hundred candles.   We **do** not believe that any other incandescent lamp would stand such a test.   The life-time of the Maxim lamp, when run at its normal power, is very long.   In plants which have been erected during the past year the average lifetime of the lamps has been considerably over a *thousand hours*, and many lamps which **have** been burning from two to three thousand hours **are** still intact.

A dynamo-machine and ninety-seven lamps **were** started in the New-York General Post-Office on March 13, 1882.   Since that time the machine has been running one hundred and forty hours per week without repairs or an accident, and on September 1st, 1882, the average record of the lamps was eighteen hundred and fifty hours each.   There were fifteen lamps which had burned continuously thirty-four hundred and fifty-six hours each, and were still in good condition.

A dynamo and fifty-six lamps were placed on the ferryboat *Jersey City* of the Pennsylvania R. R. Co., in November, 1881.   On August 29th, 1882, the plant had been in actual operation sixteen hundred and forty-five hours, and the average lifetime of the lamps was eleven hundred and nine hours each.

Our incandescent system was the first one ever put into practical commercial use. It was first introduced in the early fall of 1880, and has been in constant use since that time in the vaults of the Mercantile Safe Deposit Co., No. **120** Broadway, N. Y., in **the** New-York Stock Exchange and other places.   A large number of plants have since been erected, all of which are giving perfect satisfaction; among the places where such plants are in operation in New-York City may be mentioned the Hoffman House, the St. Nicholas Hotel, the National Park Bank, the Post-Office, and Washington Market.   The names of other parties using this system will be found among the references at the end of this pamphlet.

We manufacture incandescent lamps of different sizes, for giving a light of eight candles and upward.   Each lamp is provided with a socket or holder, as shown in the cut on page 19, which is so arranged that the lamp when in position is held firmly, but may be readily removed for renewal; and merely placing the lamp in the holder makes the necessary electrical connections.   These holders are made with or without switches, **or** keys for turning the light on and off, and of various styles, plain and ornamental.   **For** use with chandeliers and in similar places, it is frequently desirable to have the switch separate from the holder, and in a more accessible and convenient place; and a single switch will frequently suffice for **all the** lights on a chandelier.

SAFETY DEVICES

TO prevent all danger of overheating the conducting wires **by an** abnormal flow of current, an automatic cut-off is placed in each branch, **which** interrupts the circuit if from any cause the current passing becomes stronger than the wire can **safely carry**.   This consists of a strip made of an alloy which melts at a very low

Dynamo-electric Machine on Adjustable Base.

temperature,—in fact, below the boiling-point of water. This cut-off is placed in the lamp-holders and fixtures, or at other convenient points in the branch wires where ready access may be had for renewal of the fusible strips. Different forms of this

Fusible Cut-off, large size (closed).

Fusible Cut-off, large size (open).

cut-off are shown in the cuts on this page. The strips are made of different sizes, according to the current they are designed to carry. Owing to the fact that the alloy used fuses at so low a temperature, the drops of melted metal cannot ignite the most inflammable material.

FIXTURES.

WE manufacture and furnish a variety of fixtures for mounting the different parts of the apparatus. These vary according to the different circumstances under which the apparatus is to be used. Among them may be mentioned the following:

In the cut on page 21 is shown a supplementary base for the machine. This is made of hard wood, and may be constructed of any convenient height. The machine is mounted upon a sliding platform adjusted by means of a screw shown at the right. By means of this screw the belt may be tightened or loosened at will while the machine is running. This is a very desirable feature, as it entirely does away with the necessity for stopping the machine should it be necessary to tighten or slacken the belt.

In the cut at the right on this page is shown a

Fusible Cut-off, small size.

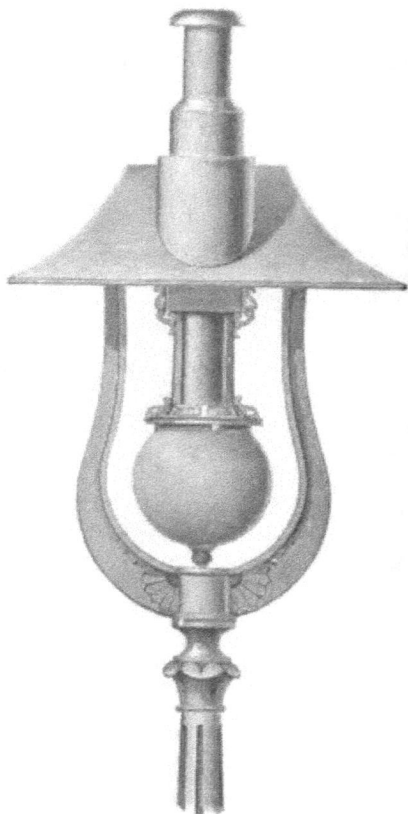

Street Lamp-post for Arc Light.

top for lamp-posts for use in street-lighting. The hood or cover at the t
of sheet-iron, and thoroughly protects the lamp from the weather, and s
time serves as a reflector. This may be applied to any form of lamp-post.

When desirable, we furnish a pulley-support for mounting arc lamps, s
that the lamp may be readily raised or lowered without interfering with the

For incandescent lamps ordinary gas-fixtures may be used by properl
the lamp-holders, and the conducting wires may be carried to the lamps with
the pipes or alongside of them. We manufacture, however, a variety of
turns for incandescent lamps.

The illustration below represents an ornamental bracket designed for in
lamps. It is so arranged that it may be swung from side to side when the

Ornamental Bracket

on, without in any way affecting the light. It can be taken down by mea
ing a thumb-nut and lifting the bracket from its wall-plate. This wall-pl
a safety device of the same character as those shown on page 37, placed i
circuit, which, in case of any abnormal flow of current, interrupts the cir
preserves the lamp from injury.

In the cut on the next page is shown a neat and simple fixture special
for use in factories, for supporting two incandescent lights. The condu
pass down inside of the fixture, and branch off on each side to the b
are arranged under opal reflectors.

We furnish fixtures, plain and ornamental, for any desired numbe
embodying these and other improvements, which specially adapt them to

ERECTION OF APPARATUS.

WE furnish line wires and all necessary material for the erection of electric lighting plants sold by us, at current market rates. All our electric lighting apparatus has been approved by the New York Board of Fire Underwriters, and we have taken pains even to go far beyond their requirements in securing *absolute safety*, both in the construction of the apparatus and in its erection.

We prefer, in all cases, to send competent and experienced men from our factory to superintend the erection of plants which we sell, charging only the time and actual expenses of the men so engaged. Where this, however, is not practicable, we furnish explicit rules for the erection of the apparatus, and insist that the purchaser shall agree to comply with them.

CENTRAL STATIONS.

OUR systems of lighting are well adapted for furnishing lights from central stations, and many of our local companies are doing a large business in the rental of lights furnished in this way. The cuts on pages 26 and 27 are views of a station erected by the Newark Electric Light and Power Company, at Newark, N. J. This company was organized in March, 1882, and, within six months, was running upwards of three hundred arc lights from its station, and orders for additional lights were received faster than they could be supplied.

The United States Illuminating Company has upwards of six hundred arc lights in operation from different stations in New-York, besides a large number of incandescent lights. The New England Weston Electric Light Company has about three hundred lights running in Boston. The Rochester Electric Light Company has about one hundred and fifty lights running at Rochester. The Citizens' Electric Light Company has a large number of lights running at Toledo, O., and various others of our local companies have similar stations.

We build special machines and lamps for lighting by the mast or tower system, in places where this system can be used to advantage.

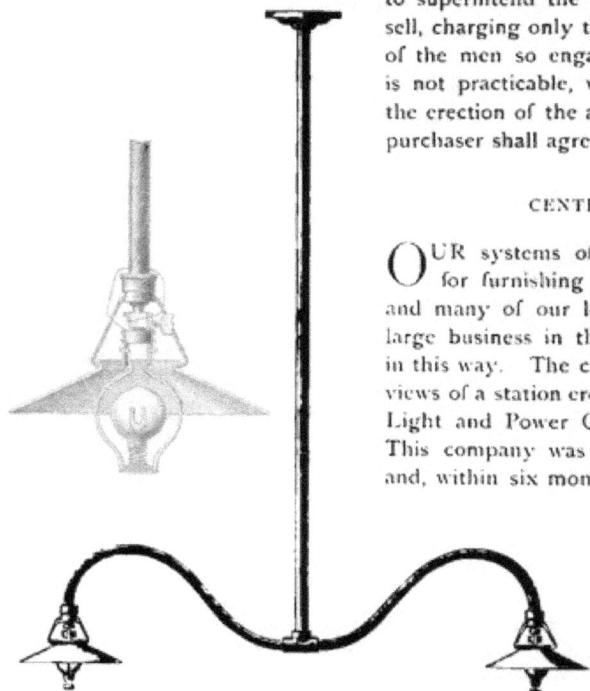

Two-light Factory Fixture.

MACHINES FOR ELECTRO-DEPOSITION OF METALS.

THE Weston Electro-depositing Machine shown in the cut on this page has achieved a wide reputation, and has in numerous competitive trials proved superior to all other machines in the market. Mr. Weston's long experience in electro-metallurgy has enabled him to adapt the machine very perfectly to the practical requirements of the business. It is very efficient in operation, strongly built, and will stand a great deal of hard usage. It needs no special skill for its proper management. A peculiar feature of this machine, of great value, is the automatic switch for preventing a reversal of the polarity of the machine. As is well known, an electro-depositing bath acts as a battery tending to produce a current in an opposite direction to the current from the machine; when the machine stops, or any accident happens to it by which its electro-motive force is reduced below the electro-motive force at the electrodes of the bath, a current flows back through the field magnets of the machine and reverses their polarity, and upon again starting the machine the direction of the current is reversed, thus removing the deposit from the articles in the bath, and in many instances, if not observed in time, destroying them and seriously injuring the solution. The automatic switch or cut-off used with this machine, which is shown in the lower right-hand

Weston Electro-depositing Machine.

corner of the cut, entirely prevents this, as it cuts the machine out of circuit upon any considerable diminution of speed. We shall shortly publish a special catalogue of this apparatus.

ELECTRIC MOTORS.

ALL of our electric light machines, especially those for running incandescent lamps, are well adapted for use as motors. We build special sizes of motors to order, fit them with regulators, and supply various other devices for a complete system of transmission of power by electricity. A special catalogue of this apparatus will also be issued soon.

PRICE-LISTS.

Price-lists will be furnished on application, giving dimensions, capacity, and other details, of all apparatus manufactured by the Company. All communications should be addressed to the general business office of the Company, Equitable Building, 120 Broadway, New-York.

1882

NEWARK ELECTRIC LIGHT & POWER Cᵒ

WESTON ELECTRIC LIGHTING STATION.

The following are some of the many testimonials received from users of our apparatus. It should be borne in mind that these testimonials relate to apparatus not embodying late improvements which render our present forms of apparatus far superior to that referred to by the writers.

TESTIMONIALS.

HALL'S SAFE AND LOCK COMPANY, MFRS. OF HALL'S PATENT SAFES AND BANK LOCKS.

CINCINNATI, September 22, 1881.

THE WESTON ELECTRIC LIGHT CO., 120 Broadway, New-York.

Gentlemen :—We have been using four of your ten-light machines for nearly one year, and find them to work in the most satisfactory manner.

We find the lights not only very powerful, but steady; the color perfectly white, which makes it very agreeable to our employees. We find it particularly adapted to our work of all classes, machine-rooms, foundries, paint and ornamental room, as also for office use. In fact, we would not be without them. Another great point about them to be considered is, the machines can be operated by the same engines in conjunction with other machinery.

We are very truly yours,

RICHARD T. PULLEN, *Secretary.*　　　　HALL'S SAFE AND LOCK COMPANY.

HALL'S SAFE AND LOCK COMPANY.

CINCINNATI, September, 4, 1882.

THE UNITED STATES ELECTRIC LIGHTING CO., New-York.

Gentlemen : We have your favor of the 30th ult. asking us in regard to the working of the lights furnished us by your company. We are now, and have been, running them full force since they were put in, and we can but reiterate our former statement that they give entire satisfaction.

We are thinking of adding to them, and wish you would let us know your best figure for a 250 light, eight candle-power, incandescent machine, etc., set up complete. Please advise at once, and oblige.

Yours truly,

R. T. PULLEN, *Secretary.*　　　　HALL'S SAFE AND LOCK COMPANY.

OFFICE OF FRASER & CHALMERS.

CHICAGO, ILL., Dec. 2, 1880.

WESTON ELECTRIC LIGHT CO., Newark, N. J.

Gentlemen : We have been using a No. 5 Weston Electric Machine and ten lights for nearly a year, and find a large saving in cost of lighting our works.

We obtain a pure white and steady light, and are satisfied in every way with the machine and lamps.

Our men like the light, and we are pleased to indorse it.

The amount of power required to run the machine, we know, is much less than those of other make.

Yours truly,

FRASER & CHALMERS.

OFFICE OF FRASER & CHALMERS.

CHICAGO, ILL., Sept. 1, 1882.

THE U. S. ELECTRIC LIGHTING CO., 120 Broadway, New York.

Gentlemen : Your favor of the 29th ult. received. The No. 5 Weston Electric Machine and ten lights that we have had in use nearly three years have given perfect satisfaction. The light we consider the most perfect we have seen, both in color and steadiness. All who have seen it are of the same opinion, and we can but say that when we increase the number of lights, which we expect to very soon, we want another machine of the same kind. We always recommend your machine as the best in the market.

Yours truly,

FRASER & CHALMERS. Per N. D. F.

FAMOUS SHOE & CLOTHING COMPANY, 705, 707, 709, 711 & 713 FRANKLIN AVENUE.

ST. LOUIS, MO., Oct. 22, 1881.

WESTON ELECTRIC LIGHT CO.

Dear Sirs : We will send you our draft, as per statement received, Monday next.

Allow us to congratulate you upon the success of your light. It is all we can expect, and if there is anything we can do for you, we are at your command.

Express us at once the following, as we have concluded to put in another ten-light machine at once (making forty lights) 1 No. 5 Generator, 12 Electric Lamps, 1,000 Feet No. 6 Line Wire, extra heavy insulation.

With our best wishes for your future success, we remain,

Yours respectfully,

FAMOUS SHOE & CLOTHING CO., JOS. SPECHT, *Manager.*

FAMOUS SHOE & CLOTHING COMPANY

ST. LOUIS, MO., September 14, 1882.

THE UNITED STATES ELECTRIC LIGHTING CO., New York.

Gentlemen : In reply to your favor asking if the lights you put in for us are still giving satisfaction, would say We have used a forty-light plant in our establishment for the past twelve months, with the most pleasing satisfaction. Your light has proven even more satisfactory than you claimed for it. During the whole time of its use we have had no trouble or mishap. We now contemplate enlarging our premises, and will want some twenty lights more.

Our gas-bills for the year previous, in the smaller house, ran as high as $4,000.00 per annum. By actual estimate the expense of illuminating the present premises (more than double as large) will not exceed $3,500.00 per year.

We are more than pleased with the result of your light, and would not part with it under any consideration.

JOS. SPECHT, *President.*

A. S. MANN & CO., DRY GOODS AND NOTION HOUSE.

ROCHESTER, N. Y., November 28, 1881.

MR. W. M. CLARK, *Gen'l Agent United States Electric Lighting Company,* Buffalo, N. Y.

Dear Sir : We have now used the electric light in our store for nearly a month, and, after the trial we have given it, we are free to say that it has more than met our expectations in its practical use for our business. We have become satisfied that it is fully adapted to our business, and, compared with any other means of lighting our store, it is invaluable.

A. S. MANN & Co.

ROCHESTER, N. Y., Aug. 16, 1882.

G. W. HEBARD, Esq., President, *The U. S. Electric Lighting Co.*, New-York.

Dear Sir : We take pleasure in stating that we have used the Weston Electric Light for lighting our store for nearly a year past. We use eight arc lights, and after the above experience we could not think of getting along without it. The light is satisfactory in every way, and from our observation of other electric lights, since introduced here, we consider ours the best light.

Yours very truly,

A. S. MANN & Co.

OFFICE OF THE IRON STEAMBOAT COMPANY.

NEW-YORK, August, 3, 1881.

THE UNITED STATES ELECTRIC LIGHTING COMPANY, 120 Broadway, City.

Gentlemen : We had one of the ten-light Weston machines, with engine complete, put on our steamer *Cetus*, at the same time we were using the Brush Light on our pier.

The success attending the lighting of this first steamer was so great that we decided at once to light the remaining boats which we had contemplated lighting, namely, the *Taurus*, *Pegasus*, and the *Cepheus*.

The color of your light is remarkable for its purity and absence of any blue shade peculiar to all others. The boats are subject to pretty rough handling in a heavy sea, yet the lights run with perfect steadiness.

Although the lights are necessarily hung quite low, the porcelain globes which your company have provided produce an effect unequaled by any other means of illumination.

The engine furnishing the lights is frequently run with 15 or 20 lbs. steam-pressure, showing the economy in the power consumed in your system.

We think that your light is well adapted to the illumination of every class of river and ocean steamers.

Yours truly,

GEO. S. SCOTT, *President.*

NEW-YORK, January, 9, 1882.

EUGENE T. LYNCH, Esq., President, *The United States Illuminating Co.*, 90 Chambers Street, City.

Dear Sir : We are so well pleased with the manner in which your company lighted four of our iron steamboats last summer, with lights of the Weston system, that we hereby order fifty-four additional lights (with necessary engines for running the same), for use upon our three remaining boats and also upon Pier 1, N. R. Your early attention to this order will oblige

Yours truly,

THE IRON STEAMBOAT CO.

A. R. WHITNEY, *Vice-President.*

NICOLL THE TAILOR.

NEW-YORK, December 1, 1881.

THE UNITED STATES ELECTRIC LIGHTING CO.

Gentlemen: I was the first to introduce the electric light in my line of business. I am glad to have the opportunity of testifying as to its efficiency and economy.

In April, 1878, I contracted with your company for six dynamo-machines and twelve lamps, which proved so satisfactory that I have since increased the number to twelve machines and twenty-four lamps.

The light enables my customers to distinguish a difference in the shade of color in goods as easily by night as in daylight, and I have always been pleased with it on the score of economy, cleanliness, and freedom from smoke and bad odors from gas.

Respectfully,

A. NICOLL.

NEW-YORK, December 17, 1881.

THE UNITED STATES ELECTRIC LIGHTING CO.

Gentlemen: I have in use at each of my theatres thirteen of your electric lights, and am highly pleased with the satisfaction they have afforded, not only to those connected with the theatres, but to the public as well.

At the time I experimented with the lights for theatre purposes, it was generally supposed that they would prove unsuitable for the lighting of an auditorium, and that they could not be utilized to the same extent as gas. I am happy to be in a position to state that all the objections urged against their use in theatres have proved unfounded, and that, at a great saving of expense and labor, they furnish a much superior light to any obtainable under the old system.

I congratulate you upon the improvements you have introduced, and look for the time when you will have reached that perfection which will in itself command your lights to general use. Until you reach that position, you can make free use of my name and theatres as a guaranty that, in your "electrics," managers and proprietors of places of public amusement will find the cheapest and best illuminating power for their purposes.

Yours, very truly,

HARRY MINER

THE NORTH CHICAGO ROLLING-MILL COMPANY

SOUTH CHICAGO, August 30, 1882.

THE UNITED STATES ELECTRIC LIGHTING CO., New-York.

Gentlemen: The work of erecting and putting in running order our electric lighting plant, begun by Mr. Young, has just been completed by Mr. Frank Radz, and, on the eve of the latter gentleman's departure, I take the opportunity, and with great pleasure in so doing, to testify to the excellent workmanship displayed by both gentlemen. Our plant of four machines and forty lamps is now entirely in operation and giving the most satisfactory results. Everything does just what was claimed for it, and the general excellence of the plant is due, I think, in a large measure to the careful and workmanlike manner in which it was put together, and the great attention paid to the slightest details. It gives me pleasure to add my testimonial of the excellence of your lighting system, and we regard ourselves as fortunate in its possession.

I am yours, very truly,

E. C. POTTER, *Superintendent*

HARTFORD, CT., September 4, 1882.

THE UNITED STATES ELECTRIC LIGHTING CO., New-York.

Gentlemen: In reply to your favor of the 30th ultimo, would say we are glad of an opportunity to express the satisfaction your lights are giving us. We have had twenty lights in operation for about a year, and are more than pleased with the results. The light is white, steady, and very powerful, and the apparatus requires very little attention. In point of economy and safety we believe it to be superior to any other system of artificial illumination.

Wishing you success, we remain, very truly yours,

THE HARTFORD ENGINEERING CO., GEO. A. BARNARD, *Manager*.

RAND, McNALLY & CO.

CHICAGO, ILL., September 1, 1882.

THE UNITED STATES ELECTRIC LIGHTING CO., Equitable Building, New-York City.

Gentlemen: Replying to yours of 8:30, we have used the Weston Arc Light nearly eighteen months, and for our press-rooms consider it invaluable and think we could hardly get along without it.

Very truly,

RAND, McNALLY & CO., *J. M. B.*

OFFICE OF THE BREMAKER MOORE PAPER COMPANY.

LOUISVILLE, KY., September 2, 1882.

THE UNITED STATES ELECTRIC LIGHTING CO., New-York.

Gentlemen: We have been using your electric light for the past two years, and find it economical, easily managed, and, in matching delicate tints after dark, indispensable. The light is steady, safe to the eyes, and our workmen are delighted with the change from gas and kerosene.

We have twelve lights, and light up our entire factory at an estimated cost of $2.50 per night, a saving of fully 50 per cent over former cost of lighting by gas.

We can cheerfully recommend it.   Yours,

BREMAKER MOORE PAPER CO., J. L. RUBEL, *Secretary*.

THE COE BRASS MANUFACTURING CO.

TORRINGTON, CT., April 19, 1882.

THE UNITED STATES ELECTRIC LIGHTING CO., New-York.

Gentlemen: In reply to your inquiry as to the fifteen lights which you put in our mills last winter, we have to say we are well satisfied with the operation of the "plant," both in quality and quantity of light obtained; it comes fully up to your representations. The light given is white, clear, and steady. It is easily managed by our mechanic, who has had no previous experience in such matters.

We do not feel the extra power required for these lights; we may use a little more fuel, but the increased consumption is so small an amount that it is hardly perceptible.

Respectfully yours,

CHARLES F. BROOKER, *Secretary*.

STEPHEN FREEMAN & SONS, MANUFACTURERS OF STEAM BOILERS AND ENGINES.

RACINE, WIS., August 17, 1882.

THE U. S. ELECTRIC LIGHTING CO., New-York.

Gentlemen: In answer to your inquiry about our electric lights now in use in our shops, we would say that the ten-light machine was run by us all last winter and gave satisfaction; so much so, indeed, that **we** now want at least one more ten-light machine to light the balance of our shops. The apparatus gives much less trouble than we expected, and does its work better than we believed it possible to do; and we can confidently say, that for work like **ours** it is invaluable. In fact, after having used it, we don't see how we ever got along without it.

Wishing you success, **we are** very **truly yours,**

S. FREEMAN & SONS.

OFFICE OF THE GLOBE WOOLEN CO.

UTICA, N. Y., September 1, 1882.

TO THE UNITED STATES ELECTRIC LIGHTING CO., **120** Broadway, **New-York.**

Gentlemen: In response to your inquiry, **I** am pleased to state that the two ten-light machines of the Weston Patent which you placed in the first floor of our main building last fall, have given entire satisfaction. The lights are uniform, powerful, and thoroughly adapted to illuminating the floor on which they are placed. In short, we are well pleased with them.

Yours truly,

ROBERT MIDDLETON, *President, M.*

THE SALEM ELECTRIC LIGHTING COMPANY, OF SALEM, MASS.

SALEM, MASS., August 28, 1882.

J. H. ALLEY, Esq., General Manager, *The New England Weston Electric Light Co.*

Dear Sir: We are using five (5) of the Weston Electric Light Dynamo-Machines, ten lights each, and for purity and brilliancy of light we consider them unsurpassed by any other system.

Yours etc.,

ARTHUR W. SHANNON, *Superintendent, The Salem Electric Light Company.*

OAKLAND GARDEN, ISAAC B. RICH, PROPRIETOR.

BOSTON, MASS., September 1, 1882.

THE NEW ENGLAND WESTON ELECTRIC LIGHT CO.

Gentlemen: With pleasure I respond **to your request** for my experience in **the use of the** Weston Electric Light.

For two seasons I have lighted the grounds of the "Oakland Garden" with your light, using ten lamps. The electric lights have added largely to the attractiveness of the Garden, and have been greatly admired by its numerous patrons. The Weston Electric Light, combining as it does the two superior qualities, clearness and steadiness, cannot fail on examination to recommend itself, and, I **can** assure you, I am pleased to testify how eminently satisfactory it has been to me.

Respectfully yours,

ISAAC B. RICH.

PLANKINTON HOUSE, MILWAUKEE, WIS., February 7, 1882.

THE U. S. ELECTRIC LIGHTING CO., **New-York.**

Gentlemen: We regard your light as **a perfect success** in our house, and will take pleasure in so stating it at any time you may wish **to refer to us.** We feel that our thanks are due to you for care exercised, and your promptness **and diligence** in giving immediate attention to all our requests.

Yours truly,

JOHN PLANKINTON.

3

OFFICE OF HAMMERSLOUGH & CO., CLOTHIERS.

KANSAS CITY, MO., July 31, 1882.

THE UNITED STATES ELECTRIC LIGHTING CO., New-York.

Gentlemen : It affords us pleasure to say that the ten-light machine we bought of you January last is giving us entire satisfaction.

Wishing you abundant success, we remain, respectfully yours,

HAMMERSLOUGH & CO.

OFFICE OF JOHN ROACH & SONS.

NEW-YORK, October 31, 1881.

THE UNITED STATES ELECTRIC LIGHTING Co., 120 Broadway, New-York.

Gentlemen : We have been using twelve of your electric lights for nearly a year at the Morgan Iron Works, Ninth Street and East River, lighting our machine-shops.

They are giving us perfect satisfaction, and our employees are enabled to **work nearly as well** by them as by daylight.

They are also very economical and safe, and require but little attention.

Yours truly.

JOHN ROACH & SONS.

OFFICE OF THE PACIFIC MAIL STEAMSHIP CO.

NEW-YORK, October 10, 1881.

THE UNITED STATES ELECTRIC LIGHTING Co., 120 Broadway, New-York.

Gentlemen : We have been using your lights on **our** pier, foot of Canal Street, for some eight months, with great success.

They are particularly adapted for our purpose, lighting up every part of the pier, and enabling us to handle our goods as well as by daylight, and with economy over gas-light, as well as greater safety from fire.

Yours truly,

W. H. LANE, *Secretary.*

OFFICE OF J. B. & J. M. CORNELL, 141 & 143 CENTRE ST.

NEW-YORK, September 22, 1881.

THE UNITED STATES ELECTRIC LIGHTING Co.

Dear Sirs : Please put in for us quick as possible one ten-light machine with **ten lamps same** as last. The one already put in by you we accept, being entirely satisfactory.

Respectfully,

J. B. & J. M. CORNELL.

OFFICE OF THE LIDGERWOOD MANUFACTURING CO., 96 LIBERTY ST., NEW-YORK.

NEW-YORK, August 19, 1881.

THE UNITED STATES ELECTRIC LIGHTING COMPANY, New-York.

Gentlemen : We wish to say that the five-light machine **and** lights recently put in for us by you at our Brooklyn shops, Erie Basin, work very satisfactorily.

Your man started it two weeks ago to-day, when it went off splendidly, and has continued to give us the same, or rather better light, every night since.

Our men that are near or in the vicinity of the lights seem to have about as good light as in **the** day-time.

Upon the whole we think it the most important improvement that we **have yet introduced** into our machine-shops to facilitate the getting of work out of a busy shop.

We shall order our light doubled soon.

Respectfully yours,

LIDGERWOOD MANUFACTURING Co., J. W. S., *Supt.*

OFFICE OF SMITH & McNELL, 198 GREENWICH ST., NEW-YORK.

NEW-YORK, September 16, 1881.

THE UNITED STATES ELECTRIC LIGHTING Co., 120 Broadway, City.

Gentlemen: We have had in use for some months in our restaurant a ten and a five-light Weston Electric Light Machine, the ten-light purchased after a trial of the five-light, and after a trial of other electric lights.

We run the five-light during the day-time, and the ten-light all night.

Our gas-bills are $85 less weekly than during the corresponding week last year, and the cost of electric lighting is simply the five horse power used during the day, and about eight-horse power at night, with the carbons, thus showing a net saving of nearly $85 per week, with the advantage of a steady, pleasing, white light, that, notwithstanding rather low ceilings, gives the greatest satisfaction to our guests, numbering over 5,000 daily.

The heat from the gas necessitated the constant **use of revolving fans, that increased the** trouble by blowing the heat down on the tables.

The care of the lights is in the hands of one of our regular help.

Gas-bills: 1880, Sept. 10—17, $187.20; 1881, Sept. 7—14, $102.05.

Yours truly,

THOS. R. McNELL.

OFFICE OF HADLEY Co., MANUFACTURERS OF SPOOL COTTONS, FINE YARNS, WARPS, HARNESS AND SEINE TWINE, ETC., ETC.

HOLYOKE, MASS., March 9, 1881.

J. H. ALLEY, Esq.

Dear Sir: Replying to your inquiry about the Weston Electric Lights at the Hadley Company's Works, I have the pleasure of saying that, so far, we have been much pleased with **them.** In fact, I may say that they have given us entire satisfaction in every respect.

Yours truly,

WM. GROVER, *Agent.*

Have now forty additional lights.

DOWNER LANDING, BOSTON HARBOR, September 6, 1880.

TO THE NEW ENGLAND WESTON ELECTRIC LIGHT Co., Boston, Mass.

Gentlemen: The Weston machines and twenty electric lights furnished by you for " Melville Gardens," Downer Landing, have been used during this season, and have proved entirely satisfactory, and are a success with us.

Yours, very respectfully,

SAMUEL DOWNER, *Proprietor of "Melville Gardens."*

[FROM THE DOWNER KEROSENE OIL CO., MANUFACTURERS OF THE PRODUCTS OF PETROLEUM. OFFICE 104 WATER STREET, NEW-YORK OFFICE, 113 MAIDEN LANE.]

BOSTON, September 6, 1880.

NEW ENGLAND WESTON ELECTRIC LIGHT CO.

Gentlemen: I take much pleasure in stating that, after some three weeks' use of your light at our works in South Boston, I am much pleased with its use. The steadiness of the light seems perfect, and the splendid illuminating quality renders our yard and its surroundings as light as day, and it is a perfect and most satisfactory means of lighting our works.

I am respectfully yours,

JOSHUA MERRILL, *Superintendent.*

THE LOWELL MANUFACTURING COMPANY, 18 SUMMER STREET.

BOSTON, MASS., December 7, 1881.

THE NEW ENGLAND WESTON ELECTRIC LIGHT CO., MOSES WILLIAMS, JR., *Treasurer.*

Dear Sir: The lights you put in at the mills of the Lowell Carpet Co. give great satisfaction. I saw them one evening last week, and I never saw any better lights. They are very steady and clear. Colors, of course, are distinguished, as they cannot be under the gas-light, and some work is now carried on by the electric light which before could only be done by daylight.

Yours truly,

ARTHUR T. LYMAN, *Treasurer.*

[FROM JAMES LEFFEL & CO., MANUFACTURERS OF DOUBLE TURBINE WATER-WHEELS AND STEAM-ENGINES. SPRINGFIELD, O.]

SPRINGFIELD, O., August 13, 1880.

WESTON ELECTRIC LIGHT CO., Newark, N. J.

Gentlemen: We have forgotten the size or number of the Weston Dynamo-Electric Machine that we have in use to light our works, for manufacturing the Leffel Turbine Water-Wheel and Bookwalter Portable Engine; but suffice it to say that, so far as we have used it, we are *perfectly* satisfied with the quality, whiteness, and steadiness of the light, and we believe there will be no occasion to use more than the five lights,—two in the foundry and three in the machine-shop. We had engaged originally of you a larger machine and more lamps, but, as we now feel, and so far as our experience goes, don't think that it will be necessary to change to the larger size, this having been put in temporarily to supply us until the larger one was completed. We could not be induced to use gas or any other kind of light as long as this holds out so well.

Yours very truly,

JAMES LEFFEL & CO.

OFFICE OF THE LEHIGH CAR MANUFACTURING CO.

STEMTON, NORTHAMPTON CO., PA., January 7, 1881.

THE WESTON ELECTRIC LIGHT CO., 29 Plane Street, Newark, N. J.

Gentlemen: We have used your electric light since February, 1880. It has given us entire satisfaction from the first, but more especially so since we are running the larger machine; we can now light up our whole works and work full hours.

The machine has already paid for itself, and we would not do without it any more at any cost.

Very respectfully,

GEO. H. STEM, *Supt.*

OFFICE OF THE BIBB MANUFACTURING CO., MACON, GA.

MACON, GA., October 1, 1881.

THE UNITED STATES ELECTRIC LIGHTING CO., 120 Broadway, New-York.

Gentlemen: We purchased of the Weston **Electric Light Company**, and put in operation some nine months since, one of their ten-light machines **in our Number One cotton-mill, and take** pleasure in saying the performance has been **highly satisfactory in quantity and quality of light,** as well as in point of economy.

We cheerfully recommend it **for cotton-mills.**

Yours very truly,

J. F. HANSON, *Agent.*

BROOKLYN, N. Y., October 26, 1881.

THE UNITED STATES ELECTRIC LIGHTING CO., 120 Broadway, New-York.

Gentlemen: We have been using one **of** your ten-light machines for several months at our theater, Adams street, Brooklyn, running ten powerful lights, some of them inside and some outside of the building, with the greatest satisfaction to ourselves and patrons.

The contrast between the color of your lights and others in use in this city is greatly in your favor. They are white and steady, resembling sunlight **more** than anything else. We are running them from a small engine and boiler, the whole apparatus taking up but very little space, and requiring but little attention.

Yours truly,

Hyde & Behman's Theater, Brooklyn, N. Y.
HYDE & BEHMAN.

OFFICE OF SMITH, GRAY & CO., WHOLESALE AND RETAIL CLOTHING DEALERS, 87 BROADWAY.

BROOKLYN, E. D., November 17, 1881.

THE UNITED STATES ELECTRIC LIGHTING CO., 120 Broadway, New York City.

Gentlemen: We purchased one **of** your ten-light machines after **our Mr. M. F. Smith had** thoroughly investigated all the different electric light systems in use in **and about New York.**

We had noticed a peculiarity in the whiteness of your light, and **we now find, after running** them for some time, that they are by far the most economical in **power consumed, and in the** quality of the light produced, of anything that we have yet seen.

We are using a comparatively small engine and boiler for running them, which gives us an opportunity of judging of the cost of the light. We find it a great improvement over gas, which we have entirely discontinued, and it gives our customers the advantage of selecting goods by night as well as by bright sunlight, thus nearly doubling the hours in which we can sell goods.

We have no hesitation in saying that your system is **by** far the best in **use.**

Yours truly,

SMITH, GRAY & CO.

OFFICE OF THE ROCKAWAY BEACH HOTEL.

ROCKAWAY BEACH, September 3, 1881.

THE UNITED STATES ELECTRIC LIGHTING CO., 120 Broadway, New-York.

Gentlemen: The ten-light Weston machine **and lamps that you put in for us some weeks ago** are running to our complete satisfaction.

Having had experience heretofore in various electric lamps, **knowing the power consumed** and care required in keeping them **in** order, we feel confident that **we have by far the best system** in existence for electric lighting.

The machine was put up at a very short notice, and is driven **from an ordinary engine on the** premises, and was turned over to our engineer within a few days **from starting, since which time** we have had no difficulty whatever in maintaining **the** lights without **interruption.**

One of the ten lights I experimentally had suspended from the ceiling of our main parlor, one of the largest in the country, and the result is past all conception. It has displaced forty-two five-feet burners (gas), giving a far steadier, more powerful, and brighter light than we have ever had in the same room.

We find the color is not at all objectionable to the ladies, the complexion remaining the same in the light, unlike all other electric lights that we know of, that give a blue, ghastly appearance.

Regarding the relative cost as compared with that of gas, a point I have hitherto been unable to ascertain, I can now give correctly, *viz.*: six of the ten lights now save me thirty-five thousand feet of gas per week, which, at the price I pay for gas, *viz.*, $3.50 per thousand, equals a saving of $122 per week, less the cost of running the entire ten lights, which is $40 per week, showing a net saving of $82 per week, with four lights to spare.

I am very respectfully yours,

O. G. BURNAP, *Manager of the Rockaway Beach Hotel.*

THE TRENTON IRON COMPANY.

TRENTON, N. J., September 5, 1882.

THE UNITED STATES ELECTRIC LIGHTING CO., New-York.

Gentlemen: We take pleasure in stating that we have had one of your Weston ten-light machines in operation at our works for several months past, and that it has operated very satisfactorily. The lamps give a good, steady light.

We expect still more satisfactory results from the double lamps which you have just put in to take the place of the single lamps originally furnished us.

Yours very respectfully,

THE TRENTON IRON CO.

OFFICE OF THE SHOVE MILLS.

FALL RIVER, MASS., September 2, 1882.

THE UNITED STATES ELECTRIC LIGHTING CO., New-York.

Gentlemen: In answer to your inquiry of August 30th, ultimo, we would say that your electric lights in our No. 2 mill have given great satisfaction, and we regard them as among the the best we know of the arc system.

Very truly,

GEO. A. CHACE, *Treas.*

MORRIS GROSS, IMPORTING TAILOR AND CLOTHIER.

TROY, N. Y., August 21, 1882.

THE UNITED STATES ELECTRIC LIGHTING CO., 120 Broadway, New-York.

Gentlemen: Will you kindly inform me if the "Otto" gas-engine will do to run my ten-light dynamo-machine?

I would say, regarding my light, that I am very well pleased with it, and believe it to be much steadier and whiter than any other I have ever seen.

Yours respectfully,

MORRIS GROSS, *Powers.*

A. E. BURKHARDT & Co., FURRIERS & HATTERS.

CINCINNATI, O., September 7, 1882.

THE UNITED STATES ELECTRIC LIGHTING CO., NEW-YORK.

Gentlemen : Your two Weston dynamo-machines and twelve lamps, which we have b
using in our retail salesroom and manufactory for the past twelve months, give such unquali
satisfaction in every respect that we will with pleasure give it our endorsement as the *lig*
power, purity, and steadiness.

Yours truly,

A. E. BURKHARDT & Co

F. & H. FRIES, COTTON AND WOOLEN MANUFACTURERS.

SALEM, N. C., September 7, 1882

THE UNITED STATES ELECTRIC LIGHTING CO., 115 BROADWAY, NEW-YORK.

Gentlemen : We duly received your favor of the 30th ultimo. We are much pleased
our electric lights and praise them on every proper occasion. We have never had any sort
trouble in managing either the machines or lamps.

Respectfully,

F. & H. FRIES.

ALDEN & LANSING.

ROCHESTER, N. Y., August 15, 1882.

MR. G. W. HEBARD, President, *The U. S. Electric Lighting Co.*

Dear Sir : We have been using one of the Weston ten-light machines since last January,
it has given general satisfaction.

The lights are powerful and steady, and color white, and have no difficulty in running it w
the same engine that runs all of our machinery, and could not possibly do without it.

Yours very truly,

ALDEN & LANSING. A.

POWERS BANKING HOUSE.

ROCHESTER, N. Y., September 10, 1882

G. W. HEBARD, Esq., Pres. *The United States Electric Lighting Co.*

Dear Sir : I have been using the Weston Electric Light for about one year, ten every ni
in Main Hall, and twenty-two nights in each week, in Art Gallery, and I am very much plea
with them. The effect of the steady, white light in the Art Gallery is very pleasant.

Yours truly,

D. W. POWERS

OFFICE OF THE PORTER MANUFACTURING CO. (Limited).

SYRACUSE, N. Y., April 20, 1881.

To whom it may concern : At the request of Mr. Teall, we cheerfully make the following statement as to our experience with the electric light : Mr. Childs and myself were appointed by the "Board of Directors" to go to New-York and examine the different electric lights.

We did so, and in our opinion the Weston light was a whiter light than the Brush. The bluish tinge, which is characteristic of the Brush light, seemed to be absent from the Weston light.

The power seemed to be much less per light with the Weston than it did with the Brush, from the indicator cards that were taken from engines running electric lights of both manufacturers.

We have been running the Weston light for about two months, and it has been running very satisfactorily, and has not caused any trouble.

And we think the estimate of three-fifths of a horse-power to a light of a so-called two thousand candle-power, would not be out of the way as a fair estimate of the actual power when in common use.

Yours truly,
THE PORTER MANUFACTURING CO. (Limited).
G. A. PORTER, *Treas.*

———

ALBANY, N. Y., July 28, 1881.

To whoever it may concern : This is to certify that we have used the Weston Electric Light Machine in our stores for the past seven months, and believe it to be the best machine for lighting purposes yet produced.

This light takes only about one-half as much power to each light as the Brush or any other machine that we know of.

We were running the Brush sixteen-light machine for Messrs. W. M. Whitney & Co. last fall, and, as near as we could ascertain, it took over twenty horse-power, while the Weston would not take over ten horse-power for the same number of lights.

We also find the Weston lights are much more powerful, and of a much better color, and steadier.

Yours respectfully,
R. STRICKLAND & CO.

———

OFFICE OF THE CONGRESS AND EMPIRE SPRING CO

SARATOGA SPRINGS, N. Y.

To THE WESTON ELECTRIC LIGHT COMPANY, 120 Broadway, New York.

Gents : The two ten-light machines, with twenty lamps, you furnished us in June last, for our Park and Spring Pavilions, we used regularly without interruption during our business season, from July 1st to September 18th, inclusive, and have given us entire satisfaction. The lights have been greatly admired by our visitors and guests, who generally pronounced them superior to all others in the steady, white, diffusive character of the light.

C. SHEEHAN, *Vice-Prest.*

———

CATARACT HOUSE.—WHITNEY, JERAULD & CO., PROPRIETORS.

NIAGARA FALLS, N. Y., November 12, 1881.

THE UNITED STATES ELECTRIC LIGHTING CO.

Gentlemen : Your favor of the 14th inst. is at hand. We have used a Weston light machine for lighting the rapids in the rear of our house, with great satisfaction to the guests of our house and ourselves. The light was considered to be very white and remarkably beautiful, and pure and brilliant,

Yours truly,
WHITNEY, JERAULD & CO.

BRIDGEPORT STEAMBOAT CO., SUPERINTENDENT'S OFFICE.

BRIDGEPORT, CT., May 22, 1882.

G. W. HEBARD, Esq., President *U. S. Electric Lighting Co.*

Dear Sir: In answer to your inquiry if the light we have is an advantage to us, and is what you represented it, I would say, that we formerly used gas in this depot, and we have been using the electric light between four and five months; and I must confess that it surpasses anything yet, and we cheerfully recommend it to all transportation companies to light their freight-houses or docks, where they are obliged to do much night-work. It facilitates our work; we can read the marks on freight packages the same as by daylight, and we find that there are less errors than formerly.

We hold and make business by giving it quick dispatch, and we think that this electric light will assist us to do this without any extra expense.

I remain, yours respectfully,

J. B. HUBBELL, *Supt.*

N. Y. STOCK EXCHANGE BUILDING COMPANY, SAFE DEPOSIT DEPARTMENT.

NEW-YORK, June 17, 1882.

THE UNITED STATES ELECTRIC LIGHTING COMPANY, 120 Broadway, New-York.

Gentlemen: In reply to your inquiry concerning the incandescent lights which you put in the vaults of the Stock Exchange about a year and a half ago, I would say they are highly satisfactory. They are perfectly steady, and give a bright, yet soft and pleasant light, being superior to gas not only in this respect, but also in the fact that they do not consume the oxygen of the air, and produce no heat of any consequence.

Yours truly,

EDWIN J. COLES, *Secy.*

SOCIAL MANUFACTURING COMPANY, GLOBE MILL.

WOONSOCKET, R. I., Jan. 10, 1882.

THE UNITED STATES ELECTRIC LIGHTING CO.

Gentlemen: We started the machine on your incandescent system on October 10, 1881, and from that date to January 9, 1882, they have run 2383½ hours. We have burned on the two machines together one hundred and seventeen lamps, and have obtained from them ample light for four looms per lamp. During the 2383½ hours eight of the lamps have burned out. The light is perfectly steady, and, from the ease with which it can be distributed, and absence from shadows and flickering, we consider it, for our purpose, much superior to the arc light. It has given us no trouble, and, so far, we are very much pleased with its operation.

Very truly,

HENRY F. LIPPITT, *Supt.*

JOHN H. DAVIS & CO., 17 WALL STREET.

NEW-YORK, June 17, 1882.

SECRETARY U. S. ELECTRIC LIGHTING CO., N. Y.

Gentlemen: In reply to your inquiry regarding your electric lights for office and dwelling-house, we beg to say that we have had them in our office for nearly a year, and that they give entire satisfaction, so much so that we have had all our gas-pipes removed. We have in all eleven burners, and the light they give is fully equal in brilliancy and steadiness to the best gas, and is free from the odor, heat, and vitiating properties of the latter. It has made a great difference in the purity of the atmosphere and general comfort of the office.

Yours truly,

JOHN H. DAVIS & CO.

Among the users of our Electric Lighting apparatus are the following :

YORK MANUFACTURING CO.	Saco,	Maine
PORTLAND ELECTRIC LIGHT CO.	Portland,	"
WORUMBO MANUFACTURING CO.	Lisbon Falls,	"
AMOSKEAG MANUFACTURING CO.	Manchester,	New Hampshire
MANCHESTER ELECTRIC LIGHT CO.	"	"
BERLIN MILLS	Berlin Falls,	"
FOREST FIBRE CO.	" "	"
VAN NESS HOUSE,	Burlington,	Vermont
W. A. WOODBURY,	"	"
LOCKWOOD MANUFACTURING CO.	East Boston,	Massachusetts
SHOVE MILLS,	Fall River,	"
BOSTON HERALD,	Boston,	"
STANDARD SUGAR REFINERY,	"	"
BOSTON RUBBER SHOE CO.	Malden,	"
PLYMOUTH CORDAGE CO.	Plymouth,	"
HADLEY CO.	Holyoke,	"
SALEM ELECTRIC LIGHT CO.	Salem,	"
LOWELL ELECTRIC LIGHT CO.	Lowell,	"
LOWELL MANUFACTURING CO.	"	"
GRAYLOCK MILLS,	North Adams,	"
MERRIMACK MANUFACTURING CO.	Lowell,	"
DOWNER KEROSENE OIL CO.	Boston,	"
OAKLAND GARDENS,	"	"
HODGE & CO.	East Boston,	"
PRANG & CO.	Boston,	"
BOSTON & ALBANY RAILROAD DEPOT,	Worcester,	"
MELVILLE GARDENS,	Downer's Landing,	"
SPRINGFIELD ELECTRIC LIGHT CO.	Springfield,	"
RENFREW MANUFACTURING CO.	Adams,	"
H. H. BIGELOW,	Worcester,	"
HINKLEY LOCOMOTIVE WORKS,	Boston,	"
CAPE ANN GRANITE CO.	Gloucester,	"
HOOSAC TUNNEL DOCK & ENGINE CO.	Boston,	"
GEORGE UPTON,	Peabody,	"
HOTEL PEMBERTON,	Hull,	"
C. H. BOCALL,	Boston,	"
BOSTON SUGAR REFINERY,	"	"
CHELSEA BEACH CO	Revere Beach,	"
RHODE ISLAND ELECTRIC LIGHT CO.	Providence,	Rhode Island
SOCIAL MANUFACTURING CO.	Woonsocket,	"
NEWPORT ELECTRIC LIGHT CO.	Newport,	"
ROCKY POINT HOTEL,	Providence,	"
PROVIDENCE TOOL CO.	"	"
RHODE ISLAND LOCOMOTIVE WORKS,	"	"
NARRAGANSETT HOTEL,	"	"
NAUGATUCK RAILROAD CO.	Bridgeport,	Connecticut
COE BRASS MANUFACTURING CO.	Torrington,	"
L. CANDEE & CO.	New Haven,	"
CONNECTICUT ELECTRIC LIGHT CO.	"	"
WALLACE & SONS,	Ansonia,	"
HARTFORD ENGINEERING CO.	Hartford,	"

Birmingham Iron Works,	Birmingham,	Connecticut
Rawitser & Bros.	Meriden,	"
Porter Manufacturing Co.	Syracuse,	New York
Van Devler's Hotel,	Coney Island,	"
Congress and Empire Spring Co.	Saratoga,	"
Cataract House,	Niagara Falls,	"
Thousand Island House,	Alexandria Bay,	"
Iron Steamboat Co.	New York City,	"
Miner's Theatre,	" " "	"
Lidgewood Manufacturing Co.	Brooklyn,	"
Nicoll the Tailor,	New York City,	"
Hoffman House,	" " "	"
L. Waterbury & Co.	Brooklyn,	"
N. Y. Central and H. R. R. R. Grain Elevator,	New-York City,	"
New-York Post-Office,	" " "	"
Pacific Mail S. S. Pier	" " "	"
Burden Iron Co.	Troy,	"
New-York Tribune,	New-York City,	"
White Star S. S. Pier,	" " "	"
United States Government,	West Point,	"
Smith, Gray & Co.	Brooklyn,	"
John Roach & Son, Morgan Iron Works,	New-York City,	"
St. Francis Xavier College,	" " "	"
Spuyten Duyvil Rolling-Mill,	Spuyten Duyvil,	"
Continental Iron Works,	Greenpoint, L. I.	"
Perry & Co.	Sing Sing,	"
Morris Gross,	Troy,	"
W. J. Wilcox & Co.	New-York City,	"
American Photo Engraving Co.	" " "	"
Globe Woolen Mill,	Utica,	"
Copake Iron Works,	Columbia Co.,	"
D. M. Osborne & Co.	Auburn,	"
Old Dominion S. S. Co.	New-York City,	"
Starin's Glen Island,	New Rochelle,	"
Paul Bauer,	Coney Island,	"
Rochester Electric Light Co.	Rochester,	"
Brooks Locomotive Works,	Dunkirk,	"
State Capitol,	Albany,	"
Feltman's Pavilion,	Coney Island,	"
Hyde & Behman,	Brooklyn,	"
Rockaway Beach Improvement Co.	Rockaway Beach,	"
Lawson H. King,	Matteawan,	"
Long Beach Hotel,	Long Beach,	"
Barlow & Deering,	Sing Sing,	"
Cornell Iron Works,	New-York City,	"
Chesebrough Manufacturing Co.	" " "	"
College of the City of New-York,	" " "	"
Falleill Iron Co.	Poughkeepsie,	"
Gutta Percha and Rubber Manufacturing Co.	New-York City,	"
Grand Union Hotel,	Saratoga,	"
Hudson River Tunnel,	New-York City,	"
Smith & McNell,	" " "	"
New-York Fire Department Repair Shops,	" " "	"
New-York Condensed Milk Co.	Brewster,	"
Port Henry Iron Ore Co.	Port Henry,	"
W. R. Strickland,	Albany,	"
Withersbees, Sherman & Co.	Port Henry,	"

Camden & Atlantic R. R. Co.	Camden,	New Jersey
Trenton Iron Works,	Trenton,	"
Clark Thread Works,	Newark,	"
B. Atha & Co.	"	"
Passaic Print Works,	Passaic,	"
Fort Lee Park and Steamboat Co.	Fort Lee,	"
Spalding & Jennings' Steel Works,	West Bergen,	"
Potter Printing Press Works,	Plainfield,	"
Geo. Richards, Dover Iron Works,	Dover,	"
Newark Electric Light and Power Co.	Newark,	"
Atlantic City Gas and Water Co.	Atlantic City,	"
Cape May Station,	Cape May,	"
Danforth Locomotive Works,	Paterson,	"
Rittenhouse Manufacturing Co.	Passaic,	"
James Martin & Co.	Philadelphia,	Pennsylvania
Sharpless & Sons,	"	"
Eclipse Lubricating Oil Co.	Franklin,	"
Catasauqua Iron Works,	Catasauqua,	"
Philadelphia Post-Office,	Philadelphia,	"
Pennsylvania Rail Road Co., Greenwich Yards,	"	"
United States Mint,	"	"
C. W. & J. Pierce,	Bristol,	"
Robert Wetherill & Co.	Chester,	"
Lehigh Car Manufacturing Co.	Stenton,	"
Colebrook Furnaces,	Lebanon,	"
John Roach & Son,	Chester,	"
Thomas Develin & Co.	Philadelphia,	"
Renovo Shops,	Renovo,	"
Pennsylvania Coal Co.	Newburg,	"
Coal Valley Coal Co.	Pittsburg,	"
Bethlehem Iron Works,	Bethlehem,	"
Cofrode & Saylor,	Pottstown,	"
Dillworth, Porter & Co. (Limited),	Pittsburg,	"
J. R. Finney,	"	"
Wyeth J. & Bro.	Philadelphia,	"
Continental Mills,	"	"
Chester Oil Co.	Chester,	"
H. Disston & Sons,	Tacony,	"
Frick & Co.	Waynesboro,	"
Geiser Manufacturing Co.	Phillipsburg,	"
Phillipsburg Electric Light and Power Co.	Philadelphia,	"
H. & D. Henry,	Norristown,	"
James Hooven & Son,	Jeanesville,	"
J. C. Haydon & Co.	Scranton,	"
Lackawanna Coal Co.	Philadelphia,	"
Public Buildings,	"	"
Atlantic Refinery, Point Breeze,	"	"
Marshall Bros., Rolling-Mill,	"	"
Jas. Rowland & Co., Rolling-Mill,	Pittsburg,	"
Wm. A. McIntosh,	Philadelphia,	"
Philadelphia M'f'g and Smelting Co.	Pottsville,	"
Pottsville Iron and Steel Co.	White Haven,	"
Thos. L. McKeen & Co.	Philadelphia,	"
F. Sachse & Son,	Pottsville,	"
Pennsylvania Diamond Drill Co.	Pittsburg,	"
The Dispatch Pub. Co.	Philadelphia,	"
Pennsylvania Woolen Mills.		

Joel J. Bailey & Co.	Philadelphia,	Pennsylvania
Wharton Switch Co.	Jenkintown,	"
Harrison, Havemeyer & Co.	Philadelphia,	"
Maxim Station,	"	"
A. H. Carroll, Mount Vernon Mills,	Baltimore,	Maryland
United States Electric Light Co.	"	"
Baltimore Daily News,	"	"
Richmond, York River & Chesapeake R. R. Co.	West Point,	Virginia
National Dredging Co.	Washington,	District of Columbia
F. & H. Fries,	Salem,	North Carolina
United States Electric Illuminating Co.	Charleston,	South Carolina
Charleston Oil Manufacturing Co.	"	"
Geo. H. Cornelson,	Orangeburg,	"
Atlanta and West Point R. R. Co.	Atlanta,	Georgia
Atlanta Cotton Factory,	"	"
Bibb Manufacturing Co.	Macon,	"
Enterprise Manufacturing Co.	Augusta,	"
Savannah, Florida & Western Rail Road,	Columbus,	"
Savannah Electric Light Co.	Savannah,	"
People's Line of Steamers,	Columbus,	"
John M. Clark & Sons,	Augusta,	"
Savannah Railway Co.	Savannah,	"
Central Rail Road & Banking Co.	"	"
G. Hunter & Son,	Jacksonville,	Florida
De Barry's Line St. John's River Steamers,	"	"
Central Oil Mills,	Selma,	Alabama
Dallas Electric Light Co.	Dallas,	Texas
Houston Electric Light & Power Co.	Houston,	"
San Antonio Electric Light Co.	San Antonio,	"
A. E. Burkhardt & Co.	Cincinnati,	Ohio
Citizens' Electric Light Co.	Toledo,	"
James Leffel & Co.	Springfield,	"
Hall's Safe & Lock Co.	Cincinnati,	"
Buckeye Engine Co.	Salem,	"
W. U. Masters,	Cleveland,	"
Whitebreast Coal & Mining Co.	"	"
H. Herrmann,	Evansville,	Indiana
South Bend Electric Co.	South Bend.	"
North Chicago Rolling-Mill Co.	Chicago,	Illinois
Palmer House,	"	"
Wells & French Co.	"	"
Crane Bros.	"	"
Willoughby, Hill & Co.	"	"
Rust & Collidge,	"	"
Haverly's Theatre,	"	"
O. R. Keith & Co.	"	"
Fraser & Chalmers,	"	"
Joliet Steel Works.	Joliet,	"
Rand, McNally & Co.	Chicago,	"
C. H. Slack,	"	"
Bennis & McAvoy Brewing Co.	"	"
Louisville Courier-Journal,	Louisville,	Kentucky
Bremaker-Moore Paper Co.	"	"
Mayberry, Pullman & Hamilton.	"	"
Weston Electric Light Co.	Lexington,	"
H. S. Falter Manufacturing Co.	St. Louis,	Missouri
J. J. Hoyt, Mercantile Trust Co.	"	"

HAMMERSLOUGH & Co.	Kansas City,	Missouri
SMITH, BEGGS & RANKIN,	St. Louis,	"
FAMOUS SHOE & CLOTHING Co.	"	"
E. JACCARD JEWELRY Co.	"	"
MISSOURI FURNACE Co.	"	"
ALOE, HERNSTEIN & Co.	"	"
ST. JOSEPH UNION DEPOT,	St. Joseph,	"
SWIFT ELECTRIC LIGHT Co.	Bay City and East Saginaw,	Michigan
HEBARD & THURBER LUMBER Co.	L'Anse,	"
GRAND TRUNK RAIL ROAD SHOPS,	Port Huron,	"
MICHIGAN CAR COMPANY SHOPS,	Detroit,	"
PENINSULAR CAR Co.	Adrian,	"
L. H. McGRAW & Co.	East Saginaw,	"
J. C. GRAM,	Au Sable,	"
J. E. POTTS,	" "	"
CARTIES & FILER,	Ludington,	"
FREEMAN S. FARR,	Muskegon,	"
F. BUSH,	Kalamazoo,	"
ST. PAUL ELECTRIC LIGHT & POWER Co.	St. Paul,	Minnesota
E. H. STEELE,	Minneapolis,	"
RED RIVER LAND AND IMPROVEMENT Co.		"
JOSEPH McKEY & Co.	St. Paul,	"
GOODNOW & HAWLEY,	Minneapolis,	"
CHIPPEWA LUMBER AND BOOM Co,	Chippewa Falls,	Wisconsin
STEPHEN FREEMAN & SONS.	Racine,	"
PLANKINTON HOUSE,	Milwaukee,	"
H. S. SUTTER,	"	"
WALKER, JUDD & VEAZIE,	Marine,	"
WHITEBREAST COAL Co.	Chariton,	Iowa
PALLISTER BROS.	Ottumwa,	"
GRANT SMELTING WORKS,	Denver,	Colorado
COLORADO MINING EXPOSITION,		"
MONTANA AND UTAH MINING Co.	Butte City,	Montana Ter.
BOSTON AND MONTANA GOLD MINING Co.	Helena,	" "
OREGON IMPROVEMENT Co.	Portland,	Oregon
GEO. W. WIDLER,	"	"
J. W. GRACE & Co.	San Francisco,	California
CALIFORNIA ELECTRICAL Co.	"	"
LIBERTY HILL CON. WATER MANUFACTURING Co.	"	"
E. ZAMBRINA,	Monterey,	Mexico
F. A. SENECAL.	Montreal,	Canada
ST. LAURENCE HALL,	"	"
MERRITON PAPER MILLS.	Merriton,	Ontario, "
L. YOUNG,	Ottawa,	" "
P. V. CARROLL,	Winnipeg,	Manitoba
PANAMA RAIL ROAD Co.	Panama,	Central America
PONVERT & Co.	Cienfuegos,	Cuba
MAXIM-WESTON ELECTRIC Co.	London,	England
H. G. MOEHRING,	Frankfort-on-Main,	Germany
L. C. GUSHEL.	Melbourne,	Australia

Factory of the United States Electric Lighting Co., Newark, N. J.

www.ingramcontent.com/pod-product-compliance
Lightning Source LLC
Chambersburg PA
CBHW021547270326
41930CB00008B/1389